Andreas Müller

Emptiness is Form
Form is Emptiness

The Heart Sutra from a nondual perspective

Imprint

Bibliografische Information der Deutschen Nationalbibliothek: Die Deutsche Nationalbibliothek verzeichnet diese Publikation in der Deutschen Nationalbibliografie; detaillierte bibliografische Daten sind im Internet über www.dnb.de abrufbar.

Copyright: 2024 Andreas Müller

Coverdesign: Vivien Thomas & Andreas Müller

Verlag:
BoD · Books on Demand GmbH, In de Tarpen 42,
22848 Norderstedt
Druck:
Libri Plureos GmbH, Friedensallee 273,
22763 Hamburg

ISBN: 978-3-7693-0586-9

Content

Preface

'The Heart Sutra from a nondual perspective' is more of a juxtaposition; an apparent comparison of two empty non-messages. Who knows how it was meant at the time.

The Heart Sutra seems to consist of (at least) two levels: one in which the circumstances of the 'teaching' are described - people sitting together and talking to each other - and one level in which the actual 'teaching' takes place.

Because of this impression, only parts are commented on. I will limit myself to the pure teachings.

What is reported here - and at best also in the words of the Heart Sutra - is astonishingly simple. So-called life is astonishingly simple.

What seems to be happening is itself - a blind dance that nobody experiences, but which is everything.

"There is no one"

There is no 'I'.

There is no 'thing', no entity that sits anywhere in our body. Neither in our heart region nor in our brain nor anywhere else in our body is there a real centre. The apparent 'I' gives itself many names:

I, presence, consciousness, awareness, spirit, individual, soul, self, self-awareness.

All these words seem to describe an experience that most people refer to and around which their lives seem to revolve.

'I need this and that.'

'If I had this and that, I would be happy.'

'If my partner was so and so.'

'If I was so and so'.

'If I were enlightened.'

This is how this apparent 'I' lives: in search of something higher, truer, more fulfilling.

More power, more money, more sex, more wisdom, more clarity, more freedom, more love, optionally also for true love, true freedom, true relief, true wealth. Everything should be true and genuine - and above all, everything should be 'for me'. This means that whatever I want to have 'more' of, I should also be able to consciously experience it.

However, this 'I' - the self that seems to do its thing in our bodies - does not exist. This spirit, this soul, this consciousness does not exist. There is no one.

Liberation is the natural end of this 'I am' experience. It is the merging of this apparent entity with the world. Both - I and world, subject and object - merge into the unknown. They dissolve into nothing: into nothing that remains and into nothing that is. Nothing new is created either. The Heart Sutra starts at this apparent point.

The Heart Sutra is not a personal message, not a teaching, not learnt wisdom. It comes, to the extent that it corresponds to 'my' message, from the direct cessation of personal energy.

This message is not folklore. Nor is it some distant

wisdom or cryptic truth spoken by wise men that can never be attained.

Natural reality is direct and uncomplicated, neither near nor far: it is exactly what appears to be happening. What seems to be happening is neither mysterious nor wise. It is neither hidden nor can it be seen from a separate point of view. It is neither enlightened nor unenlightened. It is neither clear nor unclear. What appears to be happening is simply itself.

"The Heart Sutra"

The natural reality

'Form is empty.
Emptiness is form.
Form is nothing other than emptiness.
Emptiness is nothing other than form.'

~

That you are reading these lines is not an experience. That you are reading these lines is an impersonal phenomenon that happens to no one. Reading these lines is total, complete, unknowable and at the same time empty and meaningless.

Reading these lines is the timeless and natural reality that is simply itself. Reading these lines leads nowhere, because it is already everything. Reading these lines does not point anywhere; it does not want to communicate anything, has no meaning and is not part of a personal path. There is no realisation in it and no progress either. At the same time, there is no resting in it and no stillness. The experiencer is dreamed. There is no one there who is separate from reading, from thoughts, from feelings, from its own body and from its surroundings. Everything is an undivided appearance for no one.

That is it. That is everything. That is the natural reality: what appears to be happening, what is both there and not there. Reading these lines is the form that has no content. The reading of these lines is empty and yet remains the reading of these lines.

The apparent 'I' would love to be able to look at emptiness and form separately, as if they were two aspects of a single, true reality. But that is impossible. Emptiness and form are not two. They are congruent. They are both total and yet they cancel each other out. Seen in this way, they are not even one - they are none.

Nothing really exists - really nothing at all.

Consciousness

'Sensation, discrimination, formative factors and consciousness are also empty.'

~

Nothing is real. Nothing is the experience of a real consciousness. It is this apparent I-am-consciousness that attaches the feeling of existence, the feeling of 'content', to everything. From a personal experience, it feels like living in a real 'substantial' world. It feels as if you yourself are substantial and as if what you experience is just as substantial as you are.

It is this experience that is dreamed. It is this experience that is not substantial. If the illusion of this experience fizzles out, the experience of reality itself fizzles out. Everything becomes what it has always been: timelessly empty.

But while everything turns out to be empty - empty of reality, empty of cause, empty of essence and empty of consciousness, everything remains exactly what it is. Thoughts are thoughts, feelings are feelings, trees are trees ... and so everything is already empty. The desperate search of the 'I' illusion to find a content in the world, an essence or something 'what life is really about', is concealed by the mere invention of this. It is assumed that life has a meaning, that we are 'not in this world without a reason', values and goals are invented, a deeper essence is assumed or we simply pray to a god. All this only happens in order to give one's own existence a value. All of this is done in the unconscious hope of not living in an empty and meaningless appearance.

It is part of the apparent ego illusion to experience oneself as separate and somehow as 'too much'. While the whole universe seems to be expanding in blind ignorance, the 'I' feels as if it is excluded; as if it were somehow left over and simply 'still there'. It is precisely this experience that gives rise to the impression that there are (at least) two: A world and me. As this seems insufficient, the hope of a supposed content immediately arises.

Unfortunately, there is no answer to the question of why it feels inadequate at all, except that it is what seems to be happening. It is what seems to happen that the feeling of being unfulfilled is part of the apparent ego experience. Even if from a personal perspective it feels like there is a real problem, it is simply an impression that is part of the apparent ego experience. There is no problem in life at all. There is no one at all that life has to fulfil and make happy. Life, or rather the illusionary experience of a life together with the impression of being unfulfilled, can never be transformed into a fulfilled state.

Being alive is already an appearance without content. It is empty of content, was empty of content and will always be empty of content. This emptiness is the natural reality. It is empty of content because it is everything. Every assumption of content is dreamed, or rather also without content.

An undivided appearance

*'Shariputra, in this way
all phenomena are empty:
They have no essential characteristics, they are
without generation and without cessation. They are
neither tainted nor untainted, neither diminishing
nor increasing.'*

~

What appears to happen is an undivided, apparent appearance. Nothing can be separated out of it that is actually recognisable. The impression of living in a fragmented subject-object reality is part of the impression that there is a tiny splinter called 'I'. It is this first splinter that creates the impression of fragmentation. If there is me, there are suddenly many other things that are separate from me. Things seem separate because you become aware of them: Suddenly there is me - and an experience of myself. Pure awareness, so to speak. Or in other words: pure 'I am'.

If this awareness now dares to stretch out its feelers

and direct its attention away from itself, it experiences a wide space around it. At this moment, the seemingly one - the awareness that experiences itself ('here and now') - has become two. The illusion of a subject-object reality is born. It should be noted, however, that the experience of the one self is already a subject-object experience. Funnily enough, pure awareness seems to be both the starting point (subject) and the end point (object) of its experience. One thus becomes two.

These 'two' then become 'many': A world that has one awareness at the centre of experience, around which all other objects seem to revolve, depending on how they enter awareness. Then there is 'me and my thoughts', 'me and my feelings', 'me and other people', 'me and the situation', 'me and everything else'.

Every possible way of experiencing oneself and the world is a variation of this experience, regardless of whether it is a pure self-experience or whether seemingly normal life is experienced with thoughts and feelings. Nor does it make any real difference whether joy or pain, sadness or anger are experienced. From the point of view of the apparent first-person perspective, all appear to be personal experiences.

What appears to be happening is neither 'here' nor 'now'. It is not happening at all in the sense that it is a real event. The experience of a real event is part of the illusion of the "I"-experience - here too: from the personal perspective, it seems as if something real is happening 'right now' and 'here in this place'. And just as the "I" experiences itself as being 'born', it also experiences things as having 'come into being'. It is this experience that gives everything the appearance of existence and 'being' in time and space. The sensation of 'being born' also includes the sensation of becoming and passing away, of coming and going. Both aspects are therefore part of the "I"-experience: On the one hand, there is the aspect of being and the static; on the other hand, there is the aspect of movement and process. This is why these two aspects can be found in various spiritual traditions.

For example, there are traditions that assume an eternal, unchanging, static truth - an eternal presence, an unchanging truth, God or the Absolute. Other traditions, on the other hand, cultivate the idea of permanent change. Interestingly, both ideas also contain the aspect of the Other: An eternal presence also happens 'in time' and is usually understood as a continuum, whereas permanent change also contains the unchanging.

In personal experience, this is reflected as follows: "I", the centre of awareness, am the silent centre of experience, while everything that appears in my field of awareness comes and goes.' So 'I exist while my thoughts come and go'.

Personal experience also includes the experience of right and wrong, of 'should be' and 'should not be', of 'brings me fulfilment' and 'robs me of fulfilment'. Linked to this is the hope that fulfilment can be increased or decreased.

If this experience turns out to be non-existent, all aspects of this experience fizzle out - including the feeling of being unfulfilled and the search for 'more'.

What remains is the experience itself. What remains is what appears to be happening. It is unrecognisable because it is inexperienced. It is

timeless, spaceless, indivisible, without need and
pure.

Nothing is real

'Shariputra, therefore in emptiness there is no form, no sensation, no discrimination, no formative factor, no consciousness, no eye, no ear, no nose, no tongue, no body, no mind, no form, no sound, no smell, no taste, no object of touch, and no phenomenon.'

~

Nothing really happens. There is no experience of reality. Nothing that observes, experiences, separates and categorises. There is no self that is aware. The self that believes it is experiencing itself is an appearance. It is without substance and reality and yet remains what it appears to be: an apparent illusion.

But: it is not what appears to be happening that is an illusion. It is the experience from a separate point of view that is without substance. There is no consciousness because it is inexperienced. There is no world because there is no experience of it. There is no one because there is no one. Groundless. What appears to be happening is everything - unmade, uncreated, never becoming something real.

No one knows this, because there is no one.

There is no one there

'There is no eye realm, no mind realm, and no consciousness realm. There is also no ignorance nor cessation of ignorance, to the point that there is neither old age and death nor cessation of old age and death.'

~

All conscious experience is dreamed. There is no real experience of physical seeing - there is no seer behind the eyes - nor is there a real thinker of thoughts within us. There is also no subtle entity within us.

The impression of being an unfulfilled self is dreamed. Therefore, it will never be possible to experience the end of this impression.

The whole energetic impression that there is 'something' is dreamed. There is neither a real experience nor an energy field nor a consciousness nor an experience of presence or existence. They are simply not really there.

The whole narrative of knowing and not-knowing are part of this dream. 'There is no one' means that there is no real experience and therefore no knowledge (or non-knowledge) of that experience. Nothing has begun and nothing will end.

Since nothing has been born, there is no real ageing, or experience of ageing. That 'something' is happening, that there is a real event that is taking place, is part of the dream. This experience is part of the personal presence that experiences itself as existing.

There is no one there.

Suffering is an illusion

'Similarly, there is no suffering, no origin, no cessation, no path, no original wisdom, no attainment and no non-attainment.'

~

Of course, this is where it gets exciting, because now we come to the things that interest the apparent "I" - the seeker illusion. The person does not really care whether the world is real or unreal, whether there is a coming and going or not. What they are looking for is the end of suffering - for themselves. They want to exchange their suffering experience of presence for a fulfilled experience of presence. This is exactly what it is looking for: What is suffering? Where does it come from? How can I end it? What is the truth?

All these questions come from and relate to the experience of being a separate self. Surprisingly, it is the experience of presence itself that creates the illusion of suffering - the apparent pain of separation. It was neither the unsatisfying job, the little money, the difficult partnership, nor the traumas from childhood that caused this longing for wholeness. It is the feeling of presence itself, which is accompanied by a more or less subtle pain of separation. Thus, the entire personal search serves only one purpose: to find an answer to this pain of separation. By trying to escape this pain (or to find an answer to it), the apparent ego only confirms this pain in its existence, just as it confirms itself in its existence.

Fortunately, the ego experience is not real and this seemingly deep pain of separation has no substance whatsoever. It is a phantom pain.

I call it phantom pain because although the pain appears to be tangible, its cause does not exist. And so the many thoughts and feelings, actions and non-actions that seem to come from the "I"-experience are without a real cause. Because here, too, there is no one. And both the pain of separation, the longing to heal this pain and the suffering of not being able to do so are not real in the sense that they are experienced within the apparent illusion.

Since this suffering is based on an illusion, there

will also be no end to it, at least not in the way that the apparent "I" assumes. The "I" assumes that the end of suffering lies in finding an answer to it.

This answer does not exist and will never exist. An illusionary pain - the pain of apparent separation - can never be answered in reality. Therefore, all 'healings' are nothing more than small patches - a good feeling here, an insight there and the occasional experience of unity.

There will be no such answer and, in this sense, no end to the suffering within the "I"-experience.

Realisation

'Therefore, Shariputra, since there is nothing for the Bodhisattvas to attain, they lean on and dwell in the perfection of wisdom, and their minds are without hindrance and therefore without fear.'

~

All ideas that start from a 'this is how it really is', from a great whole, an all-encompassing reality, fizzle out into nothingness. What remains is the conceptlessness of a tree. Its spirit is also without obstacles and it is also without fear. It is simply itself - without the slightest interest in itself. It has no self at all. Just like us.

The realisation we are talking about here is not a realisation at all. The fact that what appears to be happening is real and unreal, that it is perfect, that it is 'unmade', free of time, space, meaning, significance and intention, is not realised by anyone. There is no one who could and should realise this. The 'total realisation of the ultimate truth' or 'finally knowing what is actually going on here' hoped for by the "I"-illusion does not exist. There is neither the one who could, nor is there an 'ultimate truth' or 'something that is really going on'.

What appears to be happening cannot and does not have to be realised. Apparently, life lives itself - for no reason and for no one. So what is, is blind life itself - seemingly going on without anything ever happening. Apparently, there is exactly what seems to happen: whether deep sleep, the growth of trees or reconciliation after the last relationship dispute. Everything is unintentional and unconditional nothingness; a real and unreal appearance that is itself without direction.

Closing words

There is no message. There is nothing to achieve and nothing to lose. There is no one. 'I' is not real - an apparent appearance. No one is doing anything.

No one is unfulfilled. No one suffers. No one will and must experience personal fulfilment. No one will and must transcend this world and no one will find themselves in higher spheres.

This world is hell and this world is heaven. And yet it does not exist. It does not exist as it is apparently experienced: a real, tangible world for someone. Is there another world? Of course not! 'An unexperienced world' is the natural reality. Nobody lives in it. No one is separate from it. No one observes it. It is what appears to be happening. Form is empty and emptiness is form.

Source

The Heart Sutra is taken from:

https://www.tibethaus.com/fileadmin/user_upload
/Das_Herz_Sutra.pdf

Translation: Andreas Müller

Acknowledgements

Vivien Thomas

Benoît Strauss

Johannes Kelbert

Tony & Claire Parsons

About the author

Andreas was born in Ludwigsburg in 1979. After several years of spiritual searching, he met Tony Parsons in 2009.
'At first I was shocked. Although I already knew a lot and had experienced a lot, this was something new and unexpected. Suddenly, for no reason, I heard what Tony was saying. Soon it was undeniable:
There's no one there.'

Since 2011, Andreas has been giving talks and intensives all over the world.

www.thetimelesswonder.com